TEAMMATES

WRITTEN BY

PETER GOLENBOCK

DESIGNED AND ILLUSTRATED BY

PAUL BACON

GULLIVER BOOKS

HARCOURT BRACE JOVANOVICH, PUBLISHERS

San Diego   New York   London

Library of Congress Cataloging-in-Publication Data
Golenbock, Peter, 1946–
Teammates/written by Peter Golenbock;
illustrated and designed by Paul Bacon. — 1st ed.
p.   cm.
"Gulliver books."
Summary: Describes the racial prejudice experienced
by Jackie Robinson when he joined the Brooklyn Dodgers
and became the first black player in Major League baseball
and depicts the acceptance and support he received
from his white teammate Pee Wee Reese.
ISBN 0-15-200603-6
1. Robinson, Jackie, 1919–1972 — Juvenile literature.
2. Reese, Pee Wee, 1919–   — Juvenile literature.
3. Baseball players — United States — Biography — Juvenile literature.
4. Brooklyn Dodgers (Baseball team) — Juvenile literature.
[1. Robinson, Jackie, 1919–1972. 2. Reese, Pee Wee, 1919–   . 3. Baseball players.
4. Afro-Americans — Biography. 5. Race relations.] I. Bacon, Paul,
1923–   . ill. II. Title.
GV865.A1G64   1990
796.357'092 — dc20
[B]
[92]   89-38166

Printed in the United States of America
B C D E

Grateful acknowledgment is made for the use of the following:
Team photo of 1947 Brooklyn Dodgers: Courtesy of the National Baseball Library
Photo on endpaper of Jackie Robinson: From the private collection of Herb Ross
Photo on endpaper of Pee Wee Reese: From the private collection of Herb Ross
Photo of Ebbets Field: Courtesy of the National Baseball Library
Photo of Satchel Paige: Courtesy of the National Baseball Library
Baseball cards: Permission for names and likenesses: © 1989 Ty Cobb Estate under
    license authorized by Curtis Management Group, Indianapolis, IN; © 1990 Estate
    of Eleanor Gehrig under license authorized by Curtis Management Group,
    Indianapolis, IN; © 1989 Babe Ruth Baseball and the Babe Ruth Estate under
    license authorized by Curtis Management Group, Indianapolis, IN
Newspaper headlines (left to right): March 30, 1946; May 4, 1946; Dec. 15, 1945,
    Courtesy of the *Pittsburgh Courier*
Photo of Branch Rickey: Courtesy of the National Baseball Library
Photo of Jackie Robinson in Kansas City Monarchs uniform: Oct. 23, 1945, Courtesy
    of AP/Wide World Photos
Photo of Jackie Robinson and Branch Rickey: Feb. 12, 1948, Courtesy of AP/Wide
    World Photos
Sitting photo of Jackie Robinson in Dodgers uniform: From the private collection of
    Herb Ross
Aerial photo of Crosley Field: Courtesy of the Cincinnati Reds

For Charles Eliot, welcome.   And for Howard Cosell, thanks.
— P. G.

To Jack Roosevelt Robinson and Harold Reese
— P. B.

Jackie Robinson was more than just my teammate. He had a tremendous amount of talent, ability, and dedication. Jackie set a standard for future generations of ball players. He was a winner.

Jackie Robinson was also a man.

— PEE WEE REESE
October 31, 1989

Once upon a time in America, when automobiles were black and looked like tanks and laundry was white and hung on clotheslines to dry, there were two wonderful baseball leagues that no longer exist. They were called the Negro Leagues.

The Negro Leagues had extraordinary players, and adoring fans came to see them wherever they played. They were heroes, but players in the Negro Leagues didn't make much money and their lives on the road were hard.

SATCHEL PAIGE

Laws against segregation didn't exist in the 1940s. In many places in this country, black people were not allowed to go to the same schools and churches as white people. They couldn't sit in the front of a bus or trolley car. They couldn't drink from the same drinking fountains that white people drank from.

WHITE ONLY

Back then, many hotels didn't rent rooms to black people, so the Negro League players slept in their cars. Many towns had no restaurants that would serve them, so they often had to eat meals that they could buy and carry with them.

Life was very different for the players in the Major Leagues. They were the leagues for white players. Compared to the Negro League players, white players were very well paid. They stayed in good hotels and ate in fine restaurants. Their pictures were put on baseball cards and the best players became famous all over the world.

Many Americans knew that racial prejudice was wrong, but few dared to challenge openly the way things were. And many people were apathetic about racial problems. Some feared that it could be dangerous to object. Vigilante groups, like the Ku Klux Klan, reacted violently against those who tried to change the way blacks were treated.

BRANCH RICKEY

The general manager of the Brooklyn Dodgers baseball team was a man by the name of Branch Rickey. He was not afraid of change. He wanted to treat the Dodger fans to the best players he could find, regardless of the color of their skin. He thought segregation was unfair and wanted to give everyone, regardless of race or creed, an opportunity to compete equally on ballfields across America.

To do this, the Dodgers needed one special man.

Branch Rickey launched a search for him. He was looking for a star player in the Negro Leagues who would be able to compete successfully despite threats on his life or attempts to injure him. He would have to possess the self-control not to fight back when opposing players tried to intimidate or hurt him. If this man disgraced himself on the field, Rickey knew, his opponents would use it as an excuse to keep blacks out of Major League baseball for many more years.

Rickey thought Jackie Robinson might be just the man.

Jackie rode the train to Brooklyn to meet Mr. Rickey. When Mr. Rickey told him, "I want a man with the courage not to fight back," Jackie Robinson replied, "If you take this gamble, I will do my best to perform." They shook hands. Branch Rickey and Jackie Robinson were starting on what would be known in history as "the great experiment."

At spring training with the Dodgers, Jackie was mobbed by blacks, young and old, as if he were a savior. He was the first black player to try out for a Major League team. If he succeeded, they knew, others would follow.

Initially, life with the Dodgers was for Jackie a series of humiliations. The players on his team who came from the South, men who had been taught to avoid black people since childhood, moved to another table whenever he sat down next to them. Many opposing players were cruel to him, calling him nasty names from their dugouts. A few tried to hurt him with their spiked shoes. Pitchers aimed at his head. And he received threats on his life, both from individuals and from organizations like the Ku Klux Klan.

Despite all the difficulties, Jackie Robinson didn't give up.
He made the Brooklyn Dodgers team.

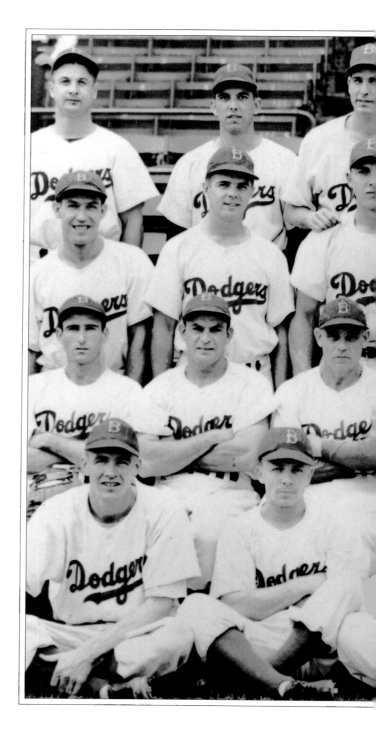

But making the Dodgers was only the beginning. Jackie had to face abuse and hostility throughout the season, from April through September. His worst pain was inside. Often he felt very alone. On the road he had to live by himself, because only the white players were allowed in the hotels in towns where the team played.

The whole time Pee Wee Reese, the Dodger shortstop, was growing up in Louisville, Kentucky, he had rarely even seen a black person, unless it was in the back of a bus. Most of his friends and relatives hated the idea of his playing on the same field as a black man. In addition, Pee Wee Reese had more to lose than the other players when Jackie joined the team.

Jackie had been a shortstop, and everyone thought that Jackie would take Pee Wee's job. Lesser men might have felt anger toward Jackie, but Pee Wee was different. He told himself, "If he's good enough to take my job, he deserves it."

When his Southern teammates circulated a petition to throw Jackie off the team and asked him to sign it, Pee Wee responded, "I don't care if this man is black, blue, or striped" — and refused to sign. "He can play and he can help us win," he told the others. "That's what counts."

CROSLEY FIELD

Very early in the season, the Dodgers traveled west to Ohio to play the Cincinnati Reds. Cincinnati is near Pee Wee's hometown of Louisville.

The Reds played in a small ballpark where the fans sat close to the field. The players could almost feel the breath of the fans on the backs of their necks. Many who came that day screamed terrible, hateful things at Jackie when the Dodgers were on the field.

More than anything else, Pee Wee Reese believed in doing what was right. When he heard the fans yelling at Jackie, Pee Wee decided to take a stand.

With his head high, Pee Wee walked directly from his shortstop position to where Jackie was playing first base. The taunts and shouting of the fans were ringing in Pee Wee's ears. It saddened him, because he knew it could have been his friends and neighbors. Pee Wee's legs felt heavy, but he knew what he had to do.

As he walked toward Jackie wearing the gray Dodger uniform, he looked into his teammate's bold, pained eyes. The first baseman had done nothing to provoke the hostility except that he sought to be treated as an equal. Jackie was grim with anger. Pee Wee smiled broadly as he reached Jackie. Jackie smiled back.

Stopping beside Jackie, Pee Wee put his arm around Jackie's shoulders. An audible gasp rose up from the crowd when they saw what Pee Wee had done. Then there was silence.

Outlined on a sea of green grass stood these two great athletes, one black, one white, both wearing the same team uniform.

"I am standing by him," Pee Wee Reese said to the world. "This man is my teammate."